Donated to Ogden LRC

Happy
Reading!

The PTC

The Sun

Dr. Raman K. Prinja

Heinemann Library
Chicago, Illinois

© 2003 Reed Educational & Professional Publishing
Published by Heinemann Library,
an imprint of Reed Educational & Professional Publishing,
Chicago, Illinois

Customer Service 888-454-2279

Visit our website at www.heinemannlibrary.com

Designed by Jo Hinton-Malivoire
Page layout by AMR
Originated by Dot Gradations Ltd.
Printed in China by W K T

07 06 05 04
10 9 8 7 6 5 4 3 2

Library of Congress Cataloging-in-Publication Data
Prinja, Raman, 1961-
    The sun / Raman Prinja.
        v. cm.
Includes bibliographical references and index.
Contents: What is the sun and why do we need it? -- What is the sun made of? -- What happens in a solar eclipse? -- What is the surface of the sun like? -- What makes the sun shine? -- Will the sun last forever? -- How do we learn about the sun?
    ISBN 1-58810-917-8 (hardcover) -- ISBN 1-40340-618-9 (pbk.)
    1. Sun--Juvenile literature. [1. Sun.] I. Title.
    QB521.5 .P75 2002
    523.7--dc21
                              2002004057

Acknowledgments
The author and publishers are grateful to the following for permission to reproduce copyright material:
p. 4/Astrophoto; p. 5/Getty Images; p. 7/Phil Cooke and Magnet Harlequi; p. 8/NHPA; p. 9/Photodisc; pp. 10, 16/NASA; pp. 11, 12,13, 15 (top and bottom), 17, 19, 20, 21, 23, 25, 26, 27, 28, 29/Science Photo Library.

Cover photograph reproduced with permission of Nasa.

The author would like to thank Kamini, Vikas, Sachin and all his family for their support.

The publisher would like to thank Geza Gyuk and Diana Challis of the Adler Planetarium for their comments in the preparation of this book.

Some words are shown in **bold,** like this. You can find out what they mean by looking in the glossary.

Contents

What Is the Sun and Why Do We Need It?

The Sun is a star, just like all those we can see twinkling at night. It looks much bigger and brighter because it is much closer to us than the other stars. The Sun is 93 million miles (150 million kilometers) away from us. The next closest star after the Sun is 270,000 times farther away! If you could travel trillions of miles out into space and look back at our Sun, it would look tiny, just like all the other stars.

The Sun is an ordinary star, like many of the others we can see in the sky at night.

The Sun, as we see it from Earth, looks yellow.

The Sun is just one star in a collection of billions of stars that make up our **galaxy,** called the Milky Way. In a galaxy like ours, the stars are held together by **gravity** in a spiral pattern. The Sun lies well away from the center of the Milky Way and is a very ordinary star. There are many stars in our galaxy that are hundreds of times bigger and millions of times more powerful. However, the Sun is the most important to us, because without it life on Earth would not exist.

A giant ball of hot gas

The Sun is a huge ball of hot, glowing gases. It is by far the brightest object seen in the sky. From Earth, the Sun appears yellow. From space or the Moon, it looks white. This is because some parts of the Sun's white light are removed when it passes through Earth's **atmosphere.** The remaining colors combine to appear yellow.

As Earth turns on its **axis,** different parts of the planet face the Sun. This is why we have day and night. Standing on Earth, it looks as if the Sun is moving across the sky during the day. But it is because Earth is spinning that the Sun appears to rise in the east and set in the west.

This movement also changes the shadows cast by sunlight. Shadows look long in the morning and evening but short at midday. Hundreds of years ago, people used **sundials** to tell time using the length and direction of shadows.

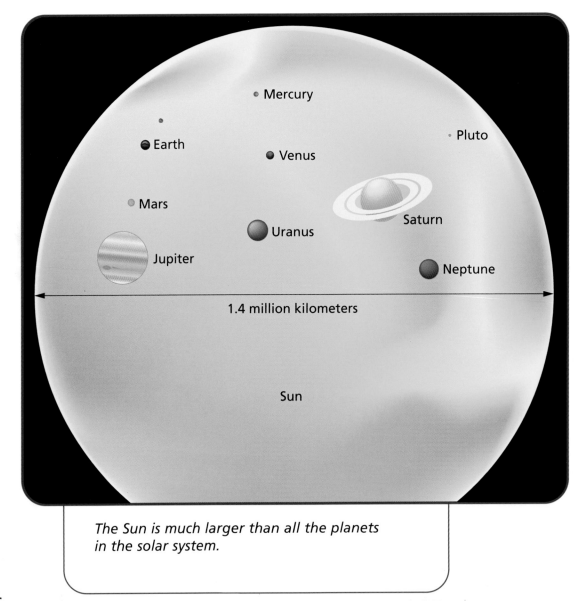

The Sun is much larger than all the planets in the solar system.

The Sun and the solar system

The Sun is the largest object in the **solar system.** The planets, moons, **asteroids,** and **comets** are the other members of the solar system. The Sun is 109 times larger than Earth. You could fit a million planets the size of Earth inside a hollow ball the size of the Sun. It is 700 times heavier than all of the planets in our solar system put together. That means the Sun has a very strong force of **gravity** that keeps all the planets **orbiting** around it. If the Sun was not there, the planets would drift out into space.

What did people think of the Sun in the past?

The Sun was very important to people in the past. Today, it still plays a special part in art, music, and religion. Many ancient civilizations worshiped some type of Sun god. More than 3,000 years ago in ancient Egypt, the Sun god was known as Ra. The Egyptians believed Ra created the world and had two children who became the **atmosphere** and the clouds on Earth. Almost 1,000 years later, the ancient Greeks believed that the Sun was the chariot of the god Helios. The chariot was driven across the heavens by four horses. Later, the Romans believed Apollo was the Sun god of light.

The Sun god, Ra, was usually painted in human form, with a falcon head.

7

*Life on Earth depends on the Sun.
It gives us light and warmth.*

We depend on the Sun

The Sun supports life on Earth by giving us light and warmth. It allows the plants we use as food to grow. The Sun's power also gives us seasons and changes our weather. Some of the fuels we use to make electricity come from plants and animals that lived millions of years ago. These plants and animals also depended on the Sun for life. When the living things died, they were slowly broken down inside Earth to make **fossil fuels** such as coal and oil.

The Sun's heat boils away some of the water from lakes and oceans, turning it into water **vapor.** This water vapor then cools and falls as the rain that plants need to grow. This process is called the **water cycle.** Plants also use the Sun's rays to turn water and **carbon** dioxide gas into food for the plants and oxygen that we need to breathe. This process is called **photosynthesis.** Without the Sun, there would be no plant or animal life on Earth.

Stonehenge

Throughout history humans have sometimes placed large stones on the ground in careful patterns. Today we believe many of these were monuments to the Sun. Stonehenge, in England, could be one example. It was built almost 5,000 years ago. Thirty very tall stones were arranged in a large circle. The ancient people might have used the giant stones to tell the time of year by watching how the Sun and Moon rose and set behind these stones.

What Is the Surface of the Sun Like?

You might think that the Sun never changes. It seems like a calm, glowing, yellow ball giving a steady stream of warmth and light. However, there is much more to the Sun than meets the eye. Just as Earth's weather is sometimes stormy, there can also be extremely violent and powerful storms on the Sun.

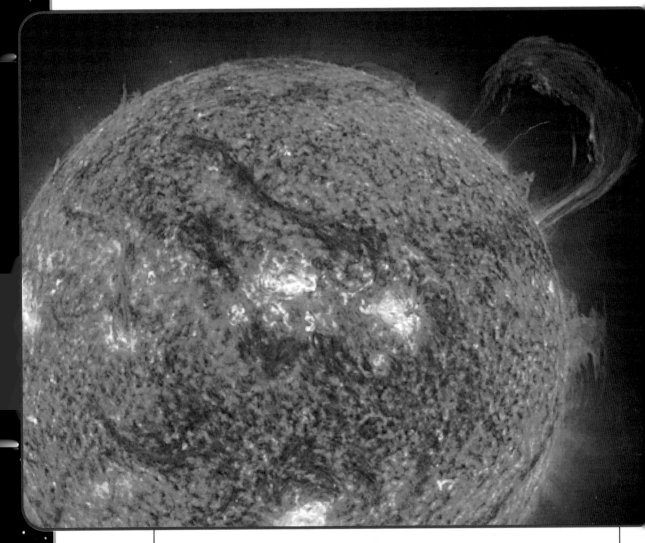

Powerful explosions and giant eruptions are seen in this picture of the Sun taken from space.

*This picture was taken using a spacecraft called SOHO. It shows huge amounts of gas streaming away from the Sun and spreading out into the **solar system**. The bright Sun itself has been blocked out. The white circle marks it.*

Powerful explosions

Huge explosions called **flares** are sometimes seen on the Sun. The gas inside a flare can have a temperature of more than 1.8 million °Fahrenheit (1 million °Celsius). If we could trap the energy from just one large flare, it would be about 40 million times greater than the energy released by a **volcano** exploding on Earth.

Giant eruptions

Storms on the Sun can also throw huge bubbles of gas out into the **solar system.** A big eruption on the Sun can send more than
11 billion tons (10 billion metric tons) of gas into space.

This loop of gas above the Sun's surface is called a **prominence.**

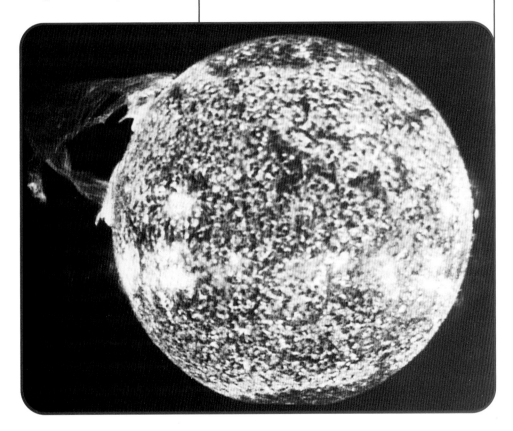

How can explosions on the Sun affect us?

The material blown off from the Sun during a storm is **electrically charged.** It can cause a huge amount of electricity to enter Earth's **atmosphere.** The **particles** arriving from the Sun can cause problems with radio and television signals. They have also caused **satellites orbiting** Earth to stop working and caused the power to go out in some cities. Because of this link between Sun storms and the Earth, scientists keep an eye on the weather in space.

Striking our planet Earth

The material from the Sun can enter Earth's atmosphere and cause **magnetic** and electrical storms. Glowing displays of light appear when electric particles from the Sun slam into the upper parts of Earth's atmosphere. We can sometimes see these displays as dazzling dances of green, blue, white, and red light in the night sky. These are known as aurora borealis (or northern lights) and aurora australis (or southern lights). The auroras are most often seen from places close to the North **Pole,** like Alaska, or near the South Pole, like Antarctica.

This aurora borealis was photographed in the night sky over Manitoba, Canada.

What Is the Sun Made Of?

Like the Earth, the Sun is made of different layers. The big difference is that the Sun's layers are all made of incredibly hot gas. The gas is mostly hydrogen and some helium.

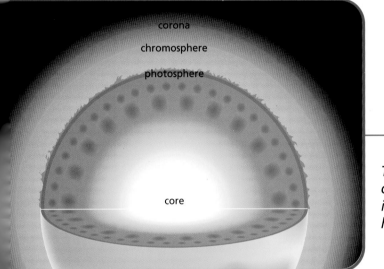

corona
chromosphere
photosphere
core

*The **core** at the center of the Sun is surrounded by hot gases.*

Layers that we can see from Earth

The Sun has three outer layers that scientists can see from our planet with powerful telescopes.

The outside layer is called the **corona.** The temperature here is over 1.8 million °Fahrenheit (1 million °Celsius) and the gas is spread very thinly. The wispy material in the corona can extend millions of miles into space.

The layer below the corona is the **chromosphere.** It is a few thousand miles thick and is made of hydrogen gas. It can have a temperature of around 18,000 °Fahrenheit (10,000 °Celsius). Violent explosions shoot beautiful loops of glowing gas called **prominences** into the chromosphere (see photo on page 12).

The lowest layer we can see is called the **photosphere.** It is only a few hundred miles thick and has a temperature of 9,900 °Fahrenheit (5,500 °Celsius). Nearly all the bright sunlight we get on Earth comes from the photosphere. Sometimes dark patches called sunspots can be seen on this layer. Sunspots appear dark because they are cooler and more **magnetic** than the surrounding regions of the Sun.

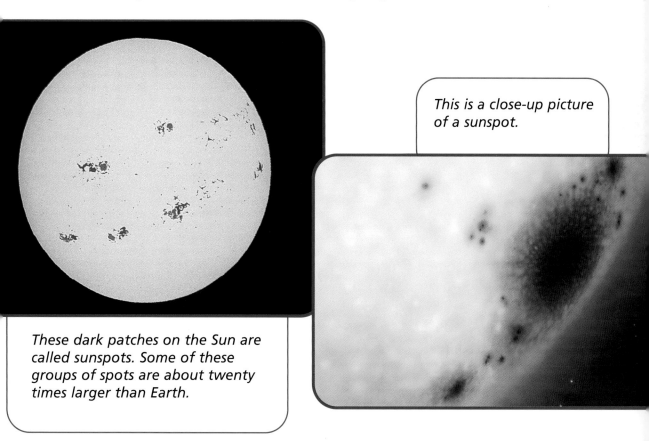

This is a close-up picture of a sunspot.

These dark patches on the Sun are called sunspots. Some of these groups of spots are about twenty times larger than Earth.

The Sun's core

At the center of the Sun, there is an incredibly hot region called the core. We cannot see into the core, but this is where the Sun's power and energy comes from.

What Makes the Sun Shine?

The Sun shines very brightly and gives off a lot of energy. If we could gather all the energy given off by the Sun in just one second, it would give the people of Europe all the electricity they need for the next 10 million years! All this energy is made in the **core** of the Sun.

An amazing power station

Like most of the stars in our **galaxy**, the Sun is made mostly of hydrogen gas. In the core of the Sun, this gas is 25 million °Fahrenheit (14 million °Celsius). The gas is very tightly squeezed together by the Sun's strong **gravity.**

In the incredible heat and pressure, the hydrogen is changed into a different gas called helium. When this happens, energy is given off. This change is called a **nuclear reaction.**

A bright Sun is seen against a dark sky from space. Astronauts on the Space Shuttle took this picture.

This picture shows the power and fury of the surface of the Sun. Huge explosions of very hot gas can be seen here. This energy comes from the core of the Sun.

All the Sun's energy comes from nuclear reactions. Every second the Sun changes 772 million tons (700 million metric tons) of hydrogen into 766 million tons (695 million metric tons) of helium. The 6 million tons (5 million metric tons) that are left over are turned into energy.

The energy from the core slowly works its way out. When it reaches the **photosphere,** we see it as brilliant sunshine. On Earth, we receive the energy from the Sun as heat and light.

What Happens in a Solar Eclipse?

The Sun is at the center of the **solar system.** Earth moves around the Sun in an **orbit** that takes one year to complete. As Earth glides around the Sun, the Moon orbits around Earth about once every month. The motion of the Moon around Earth, and Earth around the Sun can sometimes lead to special events called **eclipses.**

WARNING! – You must NEVER look directly at the Sun. Looking at the Sun can damage your eyes and can cause blindness.

A **solar** eclipse (or eclipse of the Sun) is one of the most amazing events in space that we can watch from Earth. It happens when the Moon passes directly between Earth and the Sun and blocks out the Sun's light. This only happens about once every two years. It is rare because all three objects have to be in exactly the right places.

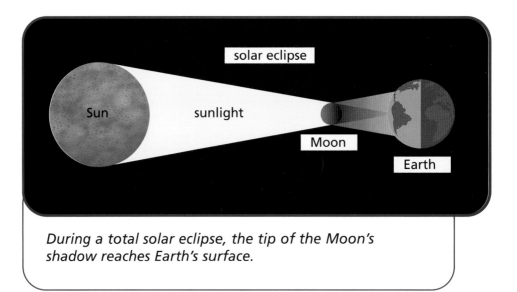

solar eclipse

Sun   sunlight

Moon

Earth

During a total solar eclipse, the tip of the Moon's shadow reaches Earth's surface.

During a total eclipse, most of the Sun's light is totally blocked by the Moon. But not all eclipses are total. When the Moon covers only a part of the Sun, some of the sunlight can get through. This is called a partial eclipse.

How can the Moon block out the Sun?

Although the Sun is 400 times larger than the Moon, the Moon looks exactly the same size as the Sun in our skies. This is because the Sun is 400 times farther away from us than the Moon. This is why the Moon can cover the whole Sun in a total eclipse.

This is a view of Earth from space during a total solar eclipse. The people that live where the Moon's shadow is hitting Earth will be able to see the eclipse best.

Try it for Yourself

To see how a solar eclipse works, get someone tall to stand a few yards away. Then, notice how you can hold up your thumb close to your eyes and block out (or eclipse) the person.

The greatest show on Earth

During a **solar eclipse,** the shadow of the Moon falls over only a small area on Earth. The darkest part of the shadow may be only about 125 miles (200 kilometers) wide. If you are lucky enough to be in the right part of the world and standing in this shadow, you will see the Sun's face completely blocked behind the Moon. It is a fantastic sight as the Moon moves slowly across the Sun.

Just before the Sun is completely covered up by the Moon, it can only shine through a few valleys between mountains on the Moon. This stage is called Bailey's beads. Seconds later, only one light beam shines through, making the Sun look like a brilliant diamond ring.

This beautiful "diamond ring" effect is seen just before the Sun's light is blocked out by the Moon.

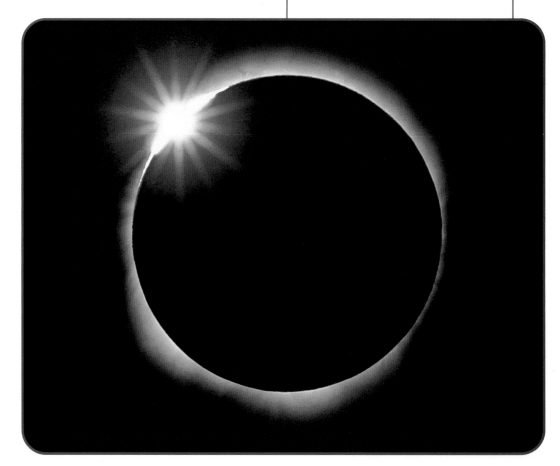

The most beautiful part of a total eclipse lasts only about two minutes. This is how long the Sun is completely hidden behind the Moon. The midday sky goes almost as dark as night. Bright stars can be seen, birds stop singing, flowers begin to close, and it gets colder. In the sky, you can see the amazing pearly white light of the Sun's **corona.** It shimmers around the outside of the Moon.

The Sun is now completely hidden behind the Moon. At this time, the amazing white light of the corona can be seen.

What Did Ancient People Think of a Solar Eclipse?

Long ago, people were frightened by eclipses. They did not understand how the light of day became night in the middle of the morning. The word *eclipse* comes from a Greek word meaning "abandonment." To abandon something means to leave it behind. They thought the Sun was abandoning Earth.

People in ancient China and ancient India thought an invisible dragon or demon was eating the Sun. During an eclipse, the Chinese would bang on pots and drums to make loud noises to frighten the dragon away. In India, people would stand in water up to their necks. They thought this act of worship would help the Sun fight off the demon. In Japan people once believed that poison dropped from the sky during an eclipse, so they covered up all their drinking wells.

Will the Sun Last Forever?

The Sun will shine steadily for a very long time but not forever. All stars live and die. These changes are very slow and happen over billions of years.

Today, our Sun is about halfway through its life. It has enough hydrogen in its **core** to keep shining for another five billion years. After that time, there will be no hydrogen left to make energy to keep the Sun going. This will be a time of major changes.

A red giant Sun

Thousands of years after its hydrogen fuel has run out, the Sun's outer layers will expand outward like a giant balloon. This will happen because of extra heat coming out of the core. At this point, the Sun will become a **red giant** star. It will swell to about a hundred times the size it is today and turn red. The Sun will be so large that it will swallow up the planet Mercury and perhaps Venus.

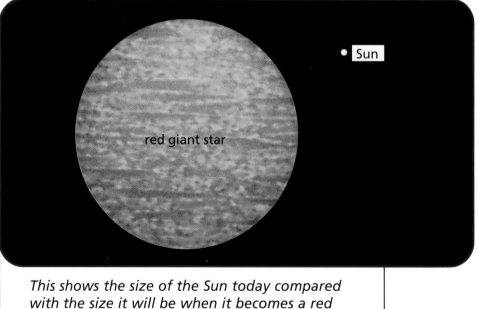

This shows the size of the Sun today compared with the size it will be when it becomes a red giant star, five billion years from now.

The death of the Sun

The outer layers of the Sun will then move far away from the star. A huge shell of gas will be shed by the Sun. This shell of gas will contain almost half of the material that makes up the Sun. The material will form a giant cloud, that will grow much larger than the whole **solar system.** This cloud is called a **planetary nebula.** When a star forms a planetary nebula, it is a sign that the star's death is very near.

This planetary nebula is many trillions of miles away from us. A dying star has thrown off its outer layers of gas. The Sun will shed a planetary nebula like this after it has turned into a red giant star.

Gravity rules

The force of **gravity** is always trying to crush the Sun. The energy made from **nuclear reactions** helps the Sun push outward to stop the squeeze of gravity. When the hydrogen fuel finally runs out, there won't be enough energy to stop the force of gravity. Gravity will win, and the **core** will get crushed into a ball the size of Earth.

After the **planetary nebula** is shed, all that will be left is a hot, tightly squeezed core. This is called a **white dwarf.** It starts off at nearly 180,000 °Fahrenheit (100,000 °Celsius), and it is made of very tightly packed **carbon** material. The carbon material is heavier than anything found on Earth. If you could bring a teaspoon of white dwarf material to Earth, it would weigh 6 tons (5 metric tons)! Over billions of years, the white dwarf will cool down into a cold, dark object that doesn't give off any light at all.

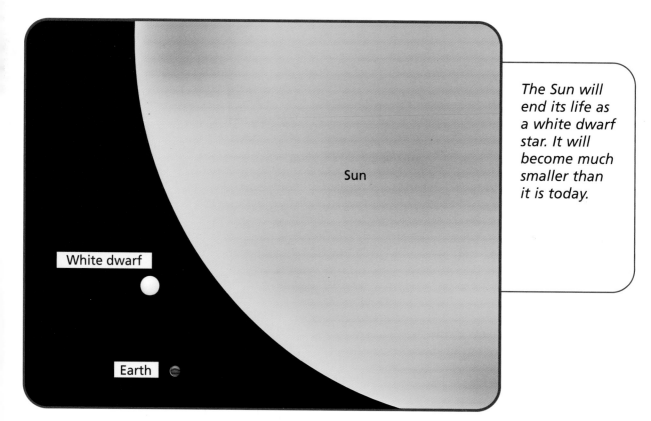

Sun

White dwarf

Earth

The Sun will end its life as a white dwarf star. It will become much smaller than it is today.

What will happen to Earth?

In about five billion years, when the Sun is a **red giant,** it will be about a hundred times the size it is now. Earth will just barely escape being swallowed up. There will be a huge, red Sun covering almost a third of our sky.

This painting shows what the Sun might look like, from Mars, when it becomes a red giant star.

The fierce heat from the huge Sun will burn all the plants and animals and boil away the oceans. The temperature on the surface of Earth will be a sizzling 1,800 °Fahrenheit (1,000 °Celsius). All life on Earth will come to an end. But don't worry, the death of the Sun, and the burning of the Earth, is billions of years away.

How Do We Learn About the Sun?

Scientists study the Sun because it is very important for life on Earth. The Sun can also teach us about the billions of other stars in our **galaxy.** There are three main ways that scientists learn about the Sun.

Using eclipses

Only during a total **eclipse** of the Sun can the outer part of the Sun, called the **corona,** be easily seen. At other times, the light from the Sun's **photosphere** is so bright that it totally outshines the corona. So, scientists take pictures and carry out many experiments during an eclipse. They are trying to find out why the corona is so hot.

Using telescopes

Far more light reaches Earth from the Sun than from any other star. **Astronomers** use giant telescopes to study the light from the Sun. They find out about the Sun's temperature and **magnetic field** and also about the different chemicals in its layers.

The largest telescope in the world used to study the Sun is the McMath solar telescope in Arizona. The telescope tower is about 100 feet (30 meters) tall.

Using spacecraft

We learn most about the Sun by using special telescopes that are launched into space. These powerful instruments are sent on spacecraft and they give the best pictures of the Sun. One of these spacecraft is called *Ulysses*, and it was the first ever to fly 124 million miles (200 million kilometers) above the north and nouth **poles** of the Sun. Another spacecraft called *SOHO* was launched in December 1995. It has sent back excellent pictures of explosions on the Sun.

The Ulysses spacecraft is seen here above Earth. It was launched into space in October 1990 to study the Sun.

Could I Ever Visit the Sun?

You could never visit the Sun because most of it is much too hot. There is also no solid place to land on; it is a gigantic ball of burning gas. To fly anywhere near the Sun you would need a spacecraft that could stand thousands of degrees. Humans could not survive the enormous heat and light from the Sun. After all, even at the safe distance of Earth, the Sun can give us sunburn if we stay out in its rays for too long.

Fact File

Here are some important facts about the Sun:

Size The Sun is almost 930,000 miles (1.5 million kilometers) across. If you think of the Sun as a basketball, then Earth would be the size of a pinhead!

Weight The Sun is 330,000 times heavier than Earth. This means the pull of **gravity** is much stronger on the Sun. Something that weighs 77 pounds (35 kilograms) on Earth would weigh 1.1 tons (1 metric ton) on the Sun.

Distance The Sun is 93 million miles (150 million kilometers) from Earth. If you imagine a car traveling from Earth at a speed of 50 miles per hour (80 kilometers per hour), it would take 214 years to reach the Sun!

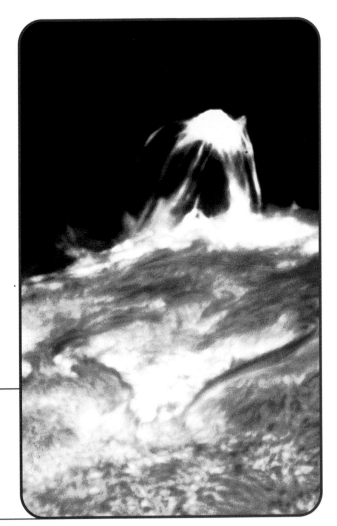

The Sun has a surface made of bubbling hot gas.

> *At sunset and sunrise, light from the Sun travels through much more of Earth's atmosphere. Blue light and other colors are removed, leaving only red, orange, and yellow for us to see.*

Temperature The Sun's **core** has a temperature of 25 million °Fahrenheit (14 million °Celsius). The upper layer of the Sun is 9,900 °Fahrenheit (5,500 °Celsius).

Spin The Sun spins on its **axis** about once every 25 days.

Age The Sun is 4.6 billion years old.

Brightness The Sun is as bright as four septillion 100-watt lightbulbs. (This huge number is written as 4 followed by 24 zeros!)

Glossary

asteroid large, rocky object in the **solar system** moving around sun

astronomer scientist who studies objects in space, such as planets and stars

atmosphere layers of gases that surround a planet

axis imaginary line around which a planet or moon spins

carbon element in all living things

chromosphere inner layer of the Sun that lies between the **photosphere** and **corona**

comet small, icy object made of gas and dust, which orbits around the Sun

core central part of an object, such as a planet or star

corona thin and extremely hot outer layer of the Sun

eclipse event during which one object passes in front of another

electrically charged full of electricity

flare powerful explosions

fossil fuel natural fuel such as coal, oil and gas

galaxy collection of billions of stars, gas, and dust

gravity force that pulls all objects toward the surface of Earth, or any other planet, moon, or star

magnetic having the ability to attract objects containing iron

magnetic field region of space affected by a **magnetic** object

nuclear reaction process where elements are joined or split

orbit path taken by an object as it moves around another body (planet or star)

particle tiny amount, or piece, of a substance

photosphere layer of the Sun from which most of the light escapes

photosynthesis process by which green plants make their food using energy from the Sun

planetary nebula cloud of gas that surrounds stars like the Sun when they run out of energy and begin to die

poles points due north and south that mark the ends of an invisible line, called the **axis,** about which a planet, moon, or star spins

prominence huge loop of gas that erupts from the Sun

red giant star that has swollen to a much larger size than the Sun is today

satellite object that revolves around a larger body (planet or star)

solar to do with the Sun

solar system group of nine planets and other objects moving around the Sun

sundial instrument that shows the time of day by using the shadow cast by sunlight

vapor the gas state of a liquid

volcano opening in a planet's surface through which hot liquid rock is thrown up

water cycle movement of water from the clouds (as rain) to the ground, rivers, lakes, and oceans, and back to into the atmosphere as vapor

white dwarf very hot small object that forms when stars like the Sun run out of energy and die

More Books to Read

Barnes, Patricia L. *Secrets of the Sun: A Closer Look at Our Star.* Austin, Tex.: Raintree/Steck/Vaughn, 2001.

Branley, Franklyn Mansfield. *The Sun: Our Nearest Star.* New York: HarperTrophy, 2002.

Walker, Niki. *The Sun.* New York: Crabtree Publishing, 2000.

Index

A GRAPHIC HISTORY OF THE CIVIL RIGHTS MOVEMENT

MARTIN LUTHER KING JR.
AND THE MARCH ON WASHINGTON

BY GARY JEFFREY
ILLUSTRATED BY NICK SPENDER

Gareth Stevens
Publishing

Please visit our website, www.garethstevens.com.
For a free color catalog of all our high-quality books,
call toll free 1-800-542-2595 or fax 1-877-542-2596.

Library of Congress Cataloging-in-Publication Data

Jeffrey, Gary.
Martin Luther King Jr. and the March on Washington / Gary Jeffrey.
p. cm. — (A graphic history of the civil rights movement)
Includes index.
ISBN 978-1-4339-7492-2 (pbk.)
ISBN 978-1-4339-7493-9 (6-pack)
ISBN 978-1-4339-7491-5 (library binding)
1. King, Martin Luther, Jr., 1929-1968. I have a dream—Juvenile literature.
2. March on Washington for Jobs and Freedom, Washington, D.C., 1963—
Juvenile literature. 3. Civil rights demonstrations—Washington (D.C.)—
History—20th century—Juvenile literature. 4. African Americans—Civil
rights—History—20th century—Juvenile literature. I. Title.
E185.97.K5J434 2013
323.1196'073—dc23
2011050608

First Edition

Published in 2013 by
Gareth Stevens Publishing
111 East 14th Street, Suite 349
New York, NY 10003

Designed by David West Books

Printed in China

CPSIA compliance information: Batch #DWS12GS: For further information contact Gareth Stevens, New York, New York at 1-800-542-2595.

CONTENTS

During the 1950s, racial segregation in public schools had been successfully challenged through the courts. However, southern states were slow to integrate, and there was still no law stopping private businesses from being as racist as they liked.

President Kennedy addresses the nation on civil rights.

A SUMMER OF (NONVIOLENT) PROTEST

In May 1963, the Southern Christian Leadership Congress, led by Martin Luther King Jr., used nonviolent protest to force businesses in Birmingham, Alabama, to desegregate. The media storm surrounding the brutality of the Birmingham police tactics against the protesters also caused President Kennedy to announce a new civil rights bill.

A MARCH FOR JOBS AND FREEDOM

The SCLC and other civil rights groups wanted to keep up the pressure for change. It was decided to organize a march on the capital to demand the civil rights bill be strengthened and passed by Congress.

The marchers would also demand a complete end to segregation in schools, passage of a bill for fair employment, and a minimum wage.

In 1942, labor leader A. Philip Randolph had the idea of marching on Washington to protest armed forces' segregation, but it didn't happen.

THE VOICE OF MORAL COURAGE

Martin Luther King Jr. was born the son of a preacher in Atlanta, Georgia, in 1929. At college, King learned about the Indian leader Gandhi, who had used nonviolent protest successfully against the British. In 1954, he became the minister of Dexter Avenue Baptist Church in Montgomery, Alabama.

When Rosa Parks famously refused to give up her place on a segregated bus and was arrested in 1955, King spearheaded the resulting Montgomery boycott campaign and became one of the foremost civil rights leaders.

A powerful speaker, Martin Luther King Jr. had the ability to inspire ordinary citizens to join together and stand up for their rights.

GETTING IT TOGETHER

The biggest question was— "Would enough people come?" Organizers toiled to publicize the march and arrange transportation. Most would come from the North, with a few brave souls from the South. Along with the other leaders, Martin Luther King Jr. worked up a speech with which to address the crowd…

Civil rights organizers set up headquarters in Washington, D.C.

MARTIN LUTHER KING JR. AND THE MARCH ON WASHINGTON

AUGUST 28, 1963, WASHINGTON, D.C.

FROM ALL OVER AMERICA THEY HAD COME. MORE THAN 250,000, MOSTLY AFRICAN AMERICAN, WITH A FEW THOUSAND WHITE SUPPORTERS JOINING THEM.

GLORY, GLORY, HALLELUJAH! GLORY, GLORY, HALLELUJAH! HIS TRUTH IS MARCHING ON.

FORWARD THEY MARCHED. FROM THE WASHINGTON MONUMENT TOWARD THE LINCOLN MEMORIAL, UNITED BY THE "BATTLE HYMN OF THE REPUBLIC."

HE IS COMING LIKE THE GLORY OF THE MORNING ON THE WAVE, HE IS WISDOM TO THE MIGHTY, HE IS SUCCOR TO THE BRAVE...

SCORES OF TELEVISION CAMERAS CAPTURED THE SCENE.

...HIS DAY IS MARCHING ON.

WNBQ

9

KING WENT ON TO DECLARE THAT 100 YEARS LATER, AFRICAN AMERICANS WERE STILL NOT FREE, AND TALKED ABOUT HOW, WITH THE DECLARATION OF INDEPENDENCE, THE FOUNDING FATHERS HAD GIVEN A **PROMISE** THAT...

...**ALL** MEN, YES, **BLACK** MEN AS WELL AS **WHITE** MEN, WOULD BE GUARANTEED THE **UNALIENABLE RIGHTS** OF LIFE, LIBERTY, AND THE PURSUIT OF HAPPINESS.

HE SAID THAT AMERICA, INSTEAD OF **HONORING** THIS PROMISE...

...HAS GIVEN THE NEGRO PEOPLE A **BAD CHECK**...

...A CHECK WHICH HAS COME BACK MARKED *"INSUFFICIENT FUNDS."*

WHILE KING REMINDED THE CROWD OF THE **URGENCY** OF THE CIVIL RIGHTS MISSION, HE ALSO COUNSELLED THEM TO BE **PEACEFUL**...

LET US NOT SATISFY OUR THIRST FOR FREEDOM BY DRINKING FROM THE CUP OF **BITTERNESS** AND HATRED.

HE REMINDED THE PROTESTERS NOT TO DISTRUST ALL WHITE PEOPLE, THAT THE TWO RACES' DESTINIES WERE **TIED TOGETHER**.

KING WENT ON TO LAY OUT HIS DREAMS FOR THE SOUTH...

...THAT THE SONS OF FORMER SLAVES AND THE SONS OF FORMER SLAVE OWNERS WILL BE ABLE TO SIT DOWN TOGETHER AT THE TABLE OF **BROTHERHOOD**.

I HAVE A DREAM TODAY...

...A DREAM THAT ONE DAY, RIGHT THERE IN ALABAMA, LITTLE BLACK BOYS AND BLACK GIRLS WILL BE ABLE TO **JOIN HANDS** WITH LITTLE WHITE BOYS AND WHITE GIRLS AS **SISTERS** AND **BROTHERS**.

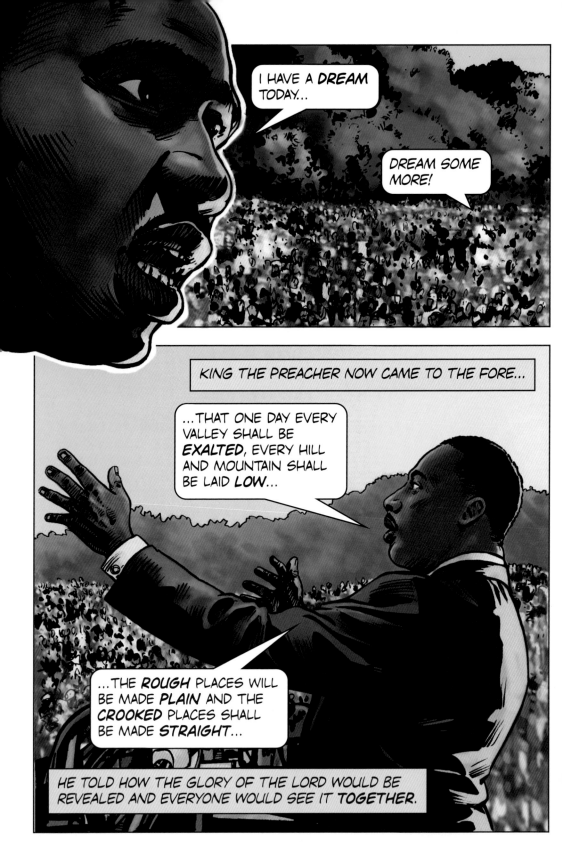

THIS IS OUR *HOPE*. THIS IS THE *FAITH* THAT I GO BACK TO THE SOUTH WITH.

WITH THIS FAITH WE WILL BE ABLE TO HEW *OUT OF* THE MOUNTAIN OF DESPAIR A *STONE* OF HOPE.

FREE AT LAST!
FREE AT LAST!
THANK GOD
ALMIGHTY, WE ARE
FREE AT LAST!

AS THESE FINAL WORDS RANG OUT, KING STEPP
DOWN TO A MIGHTY ROAR OF APPROVAL AND APP

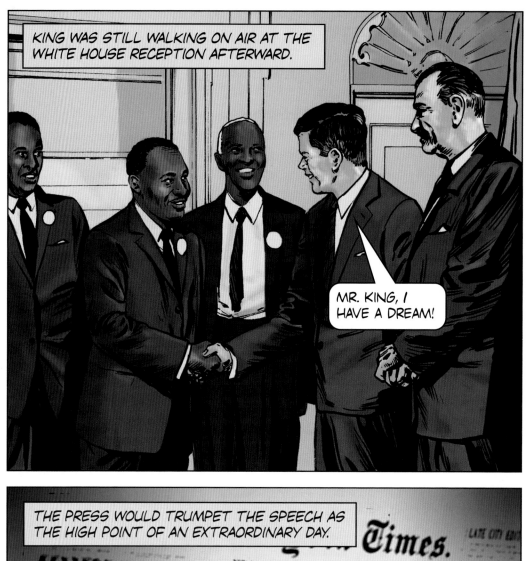

KING WAS STILL WALKING ON AIR AT THE WHITE HOUSE RECEPTION AFTERWARD.

MR. KING, I HAVE A DREAM!

THE PRESS WOULD TRUMPET THE SPEECH AS THE HIGH POINT OF AN EXTRAORDINARY DAY.

Times.

NEW YORK, THURSDAY, AUGUST 29, 1963

200,000 MARCH FOR CIVIL RIGHTS IN ORDERLY WASHINGTON RALLY; PRESIDENT SEES GAIN FOR NEGRO

The march was covered by more than 500 television cameras. King's electrifying speech was heard across the nation and did much to stir the consciences of decent white Americans both north and south.

ENDINGS AND BEGINNINGS

As his civil rights bill struggled through Congress, Kennedy was suddenly shot dead while visiting Dallas, Texas, on November 22, 1963. Vice President Lyndon B. Johnson was sworn in and vowed to get the civil rights legislation through "as a memorial to the late President."

King watches President Johnson sign the 1964 civil rights act into law. After campaigns in the Deep South, the voting rights act would follow in 1965.

MAN OF THE YEAR

King himself was made Time Magazine's Man of the Year in 1963 and awarded the Nobel Peace Prize in 1964. King continued to be a major force in the civil rights movement and was planning a mass demonstration in Washington to highlight African American poverty when he was cruelly cut down by a sniper's bullet in Memphis, Tennessee, on April 4, 1968. More than 60,000 people attended his funeral in Atlanta.

King continues to be an inspirational figure for civil rights campaigners the world over. His Washington speech is regarded as one of the greatest speeches of all time.

22

GLOSSARY

boycott To refuse to buy a product or use a service because of political reasons.

brutality Violence.

conscience A person's sense of right and wrong.

creed A set of beliefs, usually written down and recited.

emancipator One who sets people free.

rostrum A platform or podium from which speeches are delivered.

score Twenty.

segregation The forced separation of blacks and whites in public.

spearheaded Led, took charge of.

succor Support during a difficult time.

unalienable Not able to be taken away.

urgency The need to act quickly.

INDEX

B
"Battle Hymn of the Republic," 7
Birmingham, Alabama, 4
brotherhood, 15

C
Congress, 8, 22

D
Dallas, Texas, 22
Declaration of Independence, 11
Dexter Avenue Baptist Church, 5
dissatisfactions, 13

E
Emancipation Proclamation, 10

F
Founding Fathers, 11

G
Gandhi, 5

J
Jim Crow, 13
Johnson, Lyndon B., 22

K
Kennedy, President, 4, 22

L
Lincoln Memorial, 7

M
Memphis, Tennessee, 22
Montgomery, Alabama, 5

N
Nobel Peace Prize, 22

P
Parks, Rosa, 5
police brutality, 4, 13

R
Randolph, A. Philip, 4, 9, 21

S
slaves, 10
sniper, 22
Southern Christian Leadership Congress (SCLC), 4

T
Time Magazine's Man of the Year, 22

W
Washington, D.C., 4, 5, 6
Washington Monument, 7
White House, 20